Playing Sinatra

A play

Bernard Kops

Samuel French - London
New York - Toronto - Hollywood

© 1992 BY BERNARD KOPS

Rights of Performance by Amateurs are controlled by Samuel French Ltd, 52 Fitzroy Street, London W1P 6JR, and they, or their authorized agents, issue licences to amateurs on payment of a fee. **It is an infringement of the Copyright to give any performance or public reading of the play before the fee has been paid and the licence issued.**

The Royalty Fee indicated below is subject to contract and subject to variation at the sole discretion of Samuel French Ltd.

> Basic fee for each and every
> performance by amateurs   Code M
> in the British Isles

The Professional Rights in this play are controlled by DAVID HIGHAM ASSOCIATES, 5-8 Lower John Street, Golden Square, London W1R 4HA.

The publication of this play does not imply that it is necessarily available for performance by amateurs or professionals, either in the British Isles or Overseas. Amateurs and professionals considering a production are strongly advised in their own interests to apply to the appropriate agents for consent before starting rehearsals or booking a theatre or hall.

ISBN 0 573 01863 4

Please see page iv for further copyright information.

PLAYING SINATRA

First performed at the Warehouse Theatre, Croydon, on 1st October 1991, with the following cast of characters:

Norman   Ian Gelder
Sandra   Susan Brown
Phillip   Stefan Bednarczyk

The play directed by Ted Craig
Designed by Michael Pavelka

The play was subsequently presented at the Greenwich Theatre on 25th March 1992, with the same cast and director

The action takes place in a large Victorian house in Streatham, London

Time – the present

COPYRIGHT INFORMATION

(See also page ii)

This play is fully protected under the Copyright Laws of the British Commonwealth of Nations, the United States of America and all countries of the Berne and Universal Copyright Conventions.

All rights, including Stage, Motion Picture, Radio, Television, Public Reading, and Translation into Foreign Languages are strictly reserved.

No part of this publication may lawfully be reproduced in ANY form or by any means—photocopying, typescript, recording (including video-recording), manuscript, electronic, mechanical, or otherwise—or be transmitted or stored in a retrieval system, without prior permission.

Licences for amateur performances are issued subject to the understanding that it shall be made clear in all advertising matter that the audience will witness an amateur performance; that the names of the authors of the plays shall be included on all announcements and on all programmes; and that the integrity of the authors' work will be preserved.

The Royalty Fee is subject to contract and subject to variation at the sole discretion of Samuel French Ltd.

In Theatres or Halls seating Six Hundred or more the fee will be subject to negotiation.

In Territories Overseas the fee quoted in this Acting Edition may not apply. A fee will be quoted on application to our local authorized agent, or if there is no such agent, on application to Samuel French Ltd, London.

VIDEO RECORDING OF AMATEUR PRODUCTIONS

Please note that the copyright laws governing video-recording are extremely complex and that it should not be assumed that any play may be video-recorded *for whatever purpose* without first obtaining the permission of the appropriate agents. The fact that a play is published by Samuel French Ltd does not indicate that video rights are available or that Samuel French Ltd controls such rights.

SYNOPSIS OF SCENES

ACT I

SCENE 1 Late afternoon
SCENE 2 Late morning

ACT II

SCENE 1 Two weeks later. Sunday afternoon
SCENE 2 Later that night and a few days later

A licence issued by Samuel French Ltd to perform this play does not include permission to use any incidental music specified in this copy. Where the place of performance is already licensed by the Performing Right Society a return of the music used must be made to them. If the place of performance is not so licensed then application should be made to the Performing Right Society, 29 Berners Street, London W1.

A separate and additional licence from Phonographic Performances Ltd, Ganton House, Ganton Street, London W1, is needed whenever commercial recordings are used.

The extract from "Stopping by Woods on a Snowy Evening" by Robert Frost, from "The Poetry of Robert Frost" edited by Edward Connery Latham is included by permission of the Estate of Robert Frost, the Editor and Jonathan Cape as publisher.

ACT I

Scene 1

The play opens in darkness

When the Lights come up we discover a huge ramshackle and overcrowded living-room in a Victorian house in Streatham. This room also contains two spaces on either side. These are the bedrooms of Sandra and Norman Lewis

Posters and photos of Frank Sinatra are all over the place. One particular photo looms, Sinatra's face dominating everything. The house has been totally neglected and there are areas of damp on the walls. But to offset this there are also Russian and Persian wall-hangings, obvious heirlooms that could be quite valuable. Huge grotesque Chinese vases stand on sideboards. Old prints seem to cover every possible space. The furniture is huge and overwhelming. Tables, chairs and wardrobes that were obviously hand-made in immediate post-war Shoreditch. There is also an appalling three-piece suite made of pink uncut moquette

There are two sources of the music that runs throughout the action. One source is from the large radiogram, set in a mahogany cabinet. This is used when Norman and Sandra listen more deliberately to their hero singing. The other source comes from an ultra-modern CD player (perhaps the one real indulgence of our characters). This is used whenever our characters want snatches of Sinatra

There is a specific deep cupboard in the living-room. This is where Norman and Sandra keep all their packets of food, bread, drinks, utensils, crockery, etc. This cupboard also contains a microwave oven. All food that the couple prepare has been pre-cooked, bought at Marks and Spencer, and will be brought to table readiness here. The microwave will always "ping" when the food is ready. Norman and Sandra may sometimes enter this cupboard to "cook" or make tea, but we need never see the interior of this space. There is also a bookbinding workbench where Norman Lewis is usually busy, repairing the bindings of antique volumes

All in all the room contains an overbearing sense of foreboding

With the Lights we discover Norman sitting on top of his workbench, in foetal position, clutching one of his volumes

Norman (*inspecting the volume*) Fantastic! Beautiful! Half vellum. Not even Mr Zaehnsdorff could do better.

Sandra Lewis, his sister, enters. She goes to Norman and kisses him

Sandra Mr Zaehnsdorff's dead, remember? And his firm's been closed down more than twenty-five years.
Norman (*not showing surprise that she's there*) You telling me? I loved that man.
Sandra You hated him.

During this scene Norman helps Sandra off with her coat and she sits on the sofa. She is tired. He takes off her shoes, quickly takes her coat to her bedroom, whilst rummaging through her pockets. Then he returns

Norman He taught me all I know.
Sandra What's for dinner?
Norman Guess.
Sandra Something nice?
Norman You bet. Fish.
Sandra Fish? You know I hate fish.
Norman Today I am preparing something really special. Dover Sole meunière with devilled courgettes, lightly brought to perfection in butter, parsley and organic garlic. And pommes duchesse.
Sandra You know I hate fish.
Norman Fish is good for you. It goes straight to the brain.
Sandra My brain is overloaded.

Norman goes to the bureau, takes out a dagger, slowly he goes towards her plunges the dagger into her back, she screams. He laughs. It is obviously a trick dagger

Norman! I nearly died of fright. (*She laughs*) Norman! When are you going to grow up?
Norman I'm working on it Sandra.

She ruffles his hair, he replaces the dagger back in the bureau and pours two glasses of cherry brandy. Note: many of their actions together are automatic and ritualistic. As if they had been doing these things in exactly the same way for years and years

It happened again.
Sandra Oh!
Norman This morning.
Sandra Really.
Norman Yes. And this afternoon.
Sandra How many times?
Norman Three times this morning; twice this afternoon.
Sandra Did they ring off after three rings?
Norman Yes. Same as usual.
Sandra Pathetic.
Norman Did you hear them again in the night? The dogs?
Sandra Yes.
Norman It was three in the morning. Dead on. As usual.
Sandra Was it?
Norman Sandra! I consulted my clock!

Act I, Scene 1

Sandra Norman!—Dogs bark.
Norman They've got to be stopped. I phoned the police.
Sandra (*humouring him*) Did you? Good.

They toast their glasses

Oh God, I'm so whacked. (*She picks up the volume he has just bound*) You're right. It is very beautiful. It's not a book, it's a work of art.

He goes over, kisses the top of her head. She smiles and raises her hand towards him, returning the affection. Norman admires his handiwork, then he puts the book in a drawer

Norman I'm posting it off tomorrow.
Sandra You should have posted it this afternoon.
Norman I only just finished it. It had to be perfect. I'm taking it to the post office and posting it tomorrow.
Sandra You finished it on Sunday, Norman. And you really must leave the house sometimes. You must go out.
Norman What are you talking about? I love going out.
Sandra (*knowing otherwise*) Oh yes. (*Sensing his anger rising she pretends to be in pain to divert him*) Oooh!
Norman Stiff?
Sandra Please Norman!
Norman With pleasure. (*He starts to massage her neck*)
Sandra Oooh. Your hands. Magic.
Norman Yes. The hands of a bookbinder. Sensitive to all the nuances of life, contained in books. All the vagaries, the possible suffering and joy of this earthly experience. People rot but books are eternal. Are holy. Definitive. They are law, a religion unto themselves. Books are more than words. Take a typed sheet—the words are arbitrary; they carry no weight, no real validity. But now take those same words, and set them together and print them, and stitch those sheets together and bind them into a book, and presto! Suddenly those words have changed. There has been a transformation. Like the Catholic holy mass. A trans-substantiation. Now those words have authority, inevitability; have become the truth. I was privileged to be an initiate in the art of making truth. I was allowed into the inner sanctum of the craft. I'm jacking it all in next Wednesday.
Sandra Oh yeah!
Norman I'm sick of it. I've been enslaved by bloody bookbinding long enough. Good-night. That better?
Sandra Oh, Norm. That's wonderful. Take up massage.
Norman Sandra. You think I'm joking. I kid you not. I know my bookbinding has helped to keep us in cordon bleu, but enough is enough.
Sandra Norman, whatever you want is OK by me.
Norman That's what you say. But I know what you're really thinking. Well, I'm sorry, mate. I'm posting this parcel off tomorrow morning and that's the end of it.
Sandra Yes, Norman.

Norman If the game is dead let it stay dead. Why should I pretend to keep it alive? They don't want class any more; they want quiz shows.
Sandra Whatever you say, Norman.
Norman This is the age of pre-digested pap. Food. Books. Music. Show Biz. Entertainers. Singers. Only one remains. It's all gone down the drain. Nothing lasts. Everything is perishable. Nothing gets better.
Sandra Yes Norman. No Norman.
Norman This is the age of Junk. Let's all climb aboard and go down with the sinking junk. (*Pause*) That's good. Oh, that's very nice, feeling so good now. So, how's been your day?
Sandra (*laughing*) My day? Don't talk to me about my day. How should my day be?
Norman What's wrong?
Sandra Nothing.
Norman That boss again?
Sandra He's a pig.
Norman Shall I go and sort him out?
Sandra (*joking*) Yeah! With a sledge hammer.
Norman (*joking—but*) Listen. You could lure him back here—— (*He goes to the food cupboard and puts a chilled package of food into the microwave*)
Sandra Yes. I could wear alluring silver lurex to the office tomorrow.
Norman You could bring him here, ply him with Cherry Brandy, coax him into the bath, shampoo his hair until he's gurgling in bubbles. And all pink and expectant. Then I could come in with your hairdryer and drop it in the bath. Goodbye Mr Oliver McKendrick. Then we'll chop him up and mince him, and feed him to those Rottweilers.
Sandra (*laughing*) Norman! You're awful. Positively evil.
Norman Then why are you laughing?
Sandra This is better. I can actually turn my neck. I'm famished. OK, I suppose fish will have to suffice.
Norman Millions starve in Africa. She turns up her nose at Dover sole.
Sandra Is it ready?
Norman Yes. (*Consulting his watch*) Almost.
Sandra So, what are we waiting for? Norman!
Norman Sandra! The food is ready when the food is ready. Anyway, I was instructed to massage your neck. I haven't got two pairs of tentacles.
Sandra Norman! Just serve it up. I've been slaving my guts all day.
Norman So what have I been doing? Sitting on my arse? Sandra, you're too much.
Sandra I'm not enough, Norm.
Norman Why do I let you rule my life?

Pause

Sandra So what did they say?
Norman Who say?
Sandra The police.
Norman Oh. Sandra, what do they always say? Ferocious dogs outside your door? In the middle of the night sir? Rottweilers? Funny! None of your

Act I, Scene 1

neighbours seem to complain. Aren't you feeling a little persecuted sir? Nothing, but nothing will make us accept their offer. Right?
Sandra Who? (*Straining to catch up*) Oh! Yes, the developers. Norman, nothing will ever make us accept. Nothing! They'll have to carry us out.
Norman Marvellous. I'm so happy. You're absolutely resolute.
Sandra Absolutely. I've told you five thousand times.
Norman I'm sorry. I just like to hear it.

There is a "ping" from the microwave

(*Intoning as if he were a priest*) The food is ready.
Sandra So come on, make it snappy!
Norman Coming! Coming! Whatever you say, Your Majesty. Just coming.
Sandra So please make with the calories before all my body protein ebbs away.
Norman Sandra! I'm puzzled. I hate you so much. So why do I stay with you? (*He brings the packages of food from the microwave*)

They both sit down, this ritual is routine, they have been eating like this for years. They will eat straight from the packages

Sandra (*admiring the food*) Oh, that smells quite nice. (*Dipping into the fish*) In fact it tastes quite nice. Help yourself.
Norman Thank you.
Sandra You stay because you have no choice. That's the way it is.
Norman I hope you're not going out tonight.
Sandra Eat and shut up.
Norman You said you wouldn't. You promised.
Sandra Come with me then. Play bridge.
Norman Every time I think of bridge I want to throw myself off.
Sandra Splash!

They share the joke

Norman, let's have some artificial respiration.

She picks up the remote control and switches on Sinatra who sings "That Old Black Magic". They both smile and sway to the music

Norman He's wonderful. He's the best. Without him the world would be very dark. I love him. I love him so much. (*He suddenly starts to sob*)

After a few moments Sandra turns Sinatra off

Sandra (*comforting him*) Please, Norman, darling. You'll be all right. Don't worry. We'll always be together.
Norman Good. Good. Why am I like this, Sandra? Why am I so stupid?
Sandra Because you're silly. You're special.

He smiles broadly and rubs her hair

Norman We must never move from here, Sandra. Promise?
Sandra Of course. Never. Streatham may not be heaven on earth, but it's where we are; where we've always been.

Norman It's all we know; all we ever need to know. That's true, isn't it Sandra?
Sandra Absolutely, my love. Absolutely!
Norman I'm so happy. (*He is. He laughs*) Now listen. Listen carefully. What were the words that Martin Sinatra uttered——
Sandra Easy!
Norman Wait! I haven't finished the question. What were the exact words the man uttered to his young and only son Francis Albert——
Sandra It was over breakfast and his exact words were "Get outta the house and get a job!"
Norman Yes. I'll accept that.
Sandra (*sarcastically*) You'll accept that? Thank you.
Norman My pleasure. Who was the song plugger who helped Frankie right from the start?
Sandra Easy. Hank Sancola.
Norman (*with sheer glee*) Hahahahah! Wrong! Sanicola!
Sandra I know. A slip of the tongue. And he's now his personal manager.
Norman Who doesn't know that.
Sandra My turn. Listen, this is hard. Who was the classical musician——
Norman Jascha Heifitz. Frankie listened to him play the violin day after day, hour after hour. He said—quote "his constant bowing without a break, carried the melody line straight on through, just like Dorsey's trombone".
Sandra One day darling you'll be wrong and I'll be ever so happy.
Norman Never. (*Laughing*) This is all we need, isn't it?
Sandra Yes. What did he think about *My Way*?
Norman He always loathed the song, hated it like poison.
Sandra *Send in the Clowns*?
Norman He loved it. Others couldn't understand the song. He said, "I just tell them one word. 'A circus.' It's two people who have had a wonderful life and suddenly it's a circus".
Sandra (*getting a notebook from her handbag*) What did Mr Sinatra say about nature?
Norman "I believe in nature. In the birds, the sea, the sky, in everything I can see or that there is real evidence for. If these things are what you mean by God, then I believe in God."
Sandra You're remarkable.
Norman I'm the best.
Sandra One day I'm going to catch you out.
Norman You'll have to get up very early.

They kiss

I love you.
Sandra Good.
Norman (*in an American accent*) And now, ladies and gentlemen, we are privileged to have with us tonight one of Mr Sinatra's biggest fans——
Sandra Please Norm! We did it last night. Maybe later.
Norman (*angry and pleading*) Sandra! (*Again going into American*) Tell me,

Act I, Scene 1

Miss Lewis, why? What is this reverence, this love, this—obsession you have with Mr Sinatra.

Sandra knows she has to join in the game

Sandra Listen, do you want to know what I see in Mr Sinatra? Why I love him? Listen. An entry in my diary; something I wrote last night. Frankie, I love what you say about women. It's so beautiful; it's a revelation. It makes me want to cry. I quote. "I believe in giving a woman a lot of time to make up her mind about the guy she wants to spend the rest of her life with. I'm very fond of women, I admire them". Isn't that beautiful, Norman?

Norman Beautiful. So I take it that as Mr Sinatra's greatest fan you are a prominent member of his fan club.

Sandra No! I don't belong. Neither does my brother.

Norman Oh, that's odd.

Sandra No. We are true fans. We worship from afar. We don't want to share our love with anyone. I could eat him for breakfast. I just love him.

Norman Why? Why?

Sandra The glow he brings. I can be in despair and he sings and everything changes. Nobody can understand the joy I feel when he sings for me. He possesses me. Nothing else exists. All the pain of the world evaporates. People scoff. Psychiatrists dissect. But Sinatra people don't cause wars or commit acts of terrible violence. We adore him because he is unique. He is sweet and gentle. His face haunts all our lives, gives us hope, purpose. He lights up the world with his amazing yet gentle power, his voice just ignites such love inside me. I love everyone, the world, everyone. I change things. Life has meaning. I change things. Thank you.

Norman Thank you.

Sandra (*now she is American*) Tell me Mr Lewis, as his second greatest fan, what do you see in Mr Sinatra?

Norman I'm not playing any more.

His sudden mood change causes her to react. To dissipate his gathering storm clouds she goes to the radiogram and starts a record. Now they both stand close on either side of the radiogram, watching the record playing. This is "Young At Heart". They watch and listen in awe and with great concentration, happy just to observe the record actually going around. Both of them mouth Sinatra's words. Then they dance

Silence. Darkness. Sandra exits in the black-out

A short time lapse reveals Norman alone. He picks up the remote control. Sinatra sings "Strangers In The Night". Norman goes to the mirror, places a typical Sinatra hat on his head, stands back, tries to effect a typical Sinatra stance, then mouths the words of the song. Now it is as if he is singing. Then he suddenly switches the music off and looks closely in the mirror

Norman Who is the greatest entertainer that the world has ever experienced? You are. You are Frankie. There's no one else. No contest. You are the undisputed; the absolute. Thank you. Thank you very much. (*He takes off his hat*)

Dogs start to bark, the barking gets louder and louder. Norman holds his head as the barking seems to fill his brain, then he takes hold of a hammer, stands with his eyes closed. The barking subsides. He paces once or twice, then seeks some glossy magazines that have been concealed under his bed, he then sits on the sofa, opens one magazine and puts on the CD using the remote control. "The Tender Trap" plays

Suddenly there is laughter outside. It sounds like Sandra and someone else. Norman quickly stuffs the magazines under the sofa

Sandra enters, smiling

Sandra You still up.
Norman No. I'm someone else.
Sandra Oh dear, dear, dear. That was such a funny evening. You look tired. Going to bed, soon?
Norman Soon.
Sandra (*yawning*) Oooh! I'm going straight. So tired. Goodnight, Norm.
Norman Goodnight, Sarn, sleep tight. Don't let the Rottweilers bite.

She turns to go

Sandra . . .
Sandra Yes?
Norman Who saw you home?
Sandra Who saw me home? No-one.
Norman I heard you laughing. You were laughing outside the street door. You were sharing a joke.
Sandra (*minimizing*) Oh! Yes! That was Graham. You know him. He's no-one. Fancy you thinking that I could ever consider Graham. What a joke! I want to be sick. Norman, you know my attitude. You know what I think of men. You know I've never trusted them. And can you blame me? But they're not gonna get it. Not from me, they're not. Don't worry darling, you're not going to get rid of me that easily. I promise you. Nightynight. (*She goes to her room*)

Norman takes the magazines and conceals them in his room. He switches off the lights and the CD. Sandra takes out a photo album and sits on her bed. Norman now taps gently on her door

Sandra Yes, Norman, what do you want?
Norman I just wanted to say goodnight.
Sandra You said it.
Norman I want to say it again.
Sandra Say it.
Norman Good-night, Sarn.
Sandra Good-night, Norm.

But then he enters her bedroom

Act I, Scene 1

Norman Not again. You looking at that again?
Sandra (*far away*) Yes. Yes.
Norman They were so beautiful, Mum. Dad.
Sandra "The woods are lonely dark and deep, but I have promises to keep. And miles to go before I sleep".
Norman Sandra! Please!
Sandra Sorry. (*Some of this speech is in a childish voice; as if recorded in the past*) Yoohoo. Yoohoo Mummy! I've been a good girl. Please can I have an ice-cream? I promise. Daddy! I love you. More than anyone in this wide world. Catch me, Daddy. Catch me, Daddy. Look at us. How innocent. How sweet. But where are you, Norman? Why didn't you come with us? Who looked after you? Who had the courage to take you on? Don't grimace. Only joking. Can't you take a joke. They had no business, dying like that; within two weeks of each other. It's—it's sweet, but don't you just hate love birds? Imagine, still holding hands at sixty. I loved them with all my heart but they squeezed us out. Oh, look how beautiful I was. So how did I become such an ugly cow?
Norman Sandra!
Sandra Sssh!
Norman Not again.
Sandra Sssh! Look! Me on the sand. Burying Daddy's toes. Me doing cartwheels. Remember how thin I was. Like a waif. A gypsy child. Oh God, where did that sweet, smiling, mischievous girl go? She's escaped. She's upstairs somewhere, calling me, eluding me. Look! I'm as beautiful as a dream. I'm a girlie girl, remember? Why did they have to die? Why them? How could they do this to me?
Norman Don't torture yourself. When I can do it so much better for you.

She laughs. For a time they both look at the photo album in silence

Anyway, be thankful they left us this house. Without it where would we be?
Sandra On the Embankment. Anywhere. Anywhere rather than Streatham. You can't escape.
Norman What?
Sandra No matter how often you see it, it always comes out the same. Life.
Norman Sandra, I apologize.
Sandra For what?
Norman For everything I have done, and everything I have not done.
Sandra I love you, Norman.
Norman Thank you.

They kiss. He leaves her room, pretending to sleepwalk. His arms outstretched before him

Sandra Goodnight. A five-year-old boy, trapped in the body of a man. Unlike me, the child never escaped.

Norman goes to bed. Sandra gets into her bed. The Lights go out. Dogs bark. The phone rings three times. Norman laughs

Scene 2

Late morning

Norman is quietly working at his bench. Gentle Mozart plays. Norman goes to Sandra's room and frantically rummages around, searching for something. This often happens when he is alone in the house. He will also look through her pockets whenever he gets the chance. Now he finds nothing and returns to his workbench

Sandra enters from the street

Norman (*genuinely pleased*) Hello! How nice. You're home early.
Sandra I never went in.
Norman Oh?
Sandra It's such a nice day.
Norman Is it?
Sandra And it was such a magical morning. The sky crystal clear, the air like wine. I got to the West End then decided to take the day off.
Norman Good for you.
Sandra Tea?
Norman Love a cup.

Sandra is about to make tea

Hold on. Haven't you forgotten something.
Sandra Sorry. (*She goes over and kisses him*)
Norman So what did you do?
Sandra I phoned the firm. Told them I had to see the doctor about a woman's thing. That always works.
Norman So what happened after that?
Sandra I went for a stroll in Regent's Park, had a lovely cup of coffee and a croissant in the cafeteria.
Norman Very nice. (*He takes the Mozart record off and goes to the window*) You're right. It is a beautiful day. I must go out later.
Sandra We could go to the pictures.
Norman Yes. That sounds a wonderful idea. So what did you do after coffee?
Sandra Norman, where do I go when I have free time?
Norman The reference library.
Sandra Where else?
Norman Good. Anything new?
Sandra Lots.
Norman Great. Tell me.
Sandra I've turned up some really interesting early stuff.
Norman So tell me.
Sandra Later. Tonight. It'll keep. I met someone there.
Norman (*not listening*) I know! A snack! (*He looks into the cupboard*) Let's see? What do we have in stock?
Sandra I see. A snack.

Act I, Scene 2

Norman (*inspecting food packages*) I know! What about Oeufs aux Epinard? A la Findus.
Sandra Mmmmm! Wonderful.
Norman With just a little ground fresh black pepper, perhaps. And followed by fresh Provençal Raspberry Mousse?
Sandra Fabulous.

He gets busy with the food. She now needs to tell him something but seems full of trepidation

    Norman—— I met——
Norman Sandra! I clean forgot! I've written you a poem.
Sandra For me? How nice.
Norman It's called "Poodle in a Microwave".
Sandra Read it, then.
Norman "Poodle in a microwave". Here's the poem. The longest poem in the world. Here goes. "Wooof!" Like it?
Sandra (*laughing*) Is that all? Is that it?
Norman That's it. What do you think?
Sandra It's very funny and very, very wicked. Just like you.
Norman It's for you. Please put it in your pocket.
Sandra Thank you. I'm very touched.
Norman Not as touched as me.

A game is going on. A game he often plays. But she does not enjoy it

    So who was this person?
Sandra What person?
Norman The one you met in the library.
Sandra Oh yes. He was a very nice, very quiet fellow. Very spiritual, not at all physical. He's just returned from India, he says he's a seeker. He was very interesting, he knew so much about everything.
Norman Good. I like you meeting people.
Sandra (*with trepidation*) I asked him to pop round later. He said he might.
Norman Oh?
Sandra Do you mind.
Norman 'Course not.
Sandra I can always phone him; tell him not to.
Norman You've got his phone number?
Sandra (*avoiding*) He's very different from anyone I ever met. He lives over the other side, across the great divide, in West Hampstead.
Norman Ah, that explains it.
Sandra He also owns a house in Brighton.
Norman Oh, a man of property. What does he do for a living?
Sandra I didn't ask. He's obviously a man of some means. He's been travelling in Asia for some time. Seems to know a great deal about Eastern philosophy and mystical things.
Norman What does he think about F.S.?
Sandra As a matter of fact it was almost the first question I asked. I said, Mr de Groot, do you have any feeling about Frank Sinatra?

Norman And?
Sandra He said—I wrote down his very words on my way home. (*She reads from a small notebook*) "He's the greatest. He's number one."
Norman A man of taste ... I'm sure Mr Sinatra will be most relieved that Mr de Groot approves.
Sandra Norman! You really don't mind him coming round?
Norman Good lord, we can do with pleasant company.
Sandra You said it. I thought it would be a breath of fresh air. I told him you make lovely food. He said he couldn't wait.
Norman Excellent. What's his name?
Sandra Phillip de Groot.
Norman Mmm. Sounds aristocratic. (*Busy preparing the snack in the microwave*) "Microwave! Microwave! I sing of thee! You've brought Cordon Bleu cooking to crusty old batchelors like me!"

Sandra presses the remote control. Sinatra sings "Come Fly With Me"

I'm ever so pleased he loves Frankie.
Sandra So am I. I couldn't have invited him here otherwise. I told him we play Sinatra all the time. Know what he said? "Playing Sinatra means you can walk out of yourself. You can fly to the stars, and dream you are loved and happy and are wanted."
Norman He said that?
Sandra Yes, isn't that beautiful?

The microwave pings

Norman Come and get it.
Sandra I told him we play Sinatra in every way possible. CD. Records. Videos. He said, "Sinatra on tap. What can be better".

Norman brings the food packages. They both sit down and eat silently

Are you sure you're not angry?
Norman Why on earth should I be angry?
Sandra Why do you answer a question with a question?
Norman Do I? (*Laughter*) I'm sorry.
Sandra Stop apologizing.
Norman I'm sorry. (*Again laughter*)
Sandra So you don't mind me inviting him here?
Norman Am I such an ogre?
Sandra No. You're beautiful. And these eggs are out of this world. Mmmmmm!
Norman Enjoy! Enjoy!
Sandra You are the top microwave chef in the whole world.
Norman And you are the prettiest girl in Streatham.
Sandra But I must do my hair. I look an absolute mess. What would I do without you?

Suddenly the doorbell shrills through the house

Who can that be? (*She switches off the CD*)

Act I, Scene 2

Norman We don't want any, whoever it is. We're all full up with everything. People! Mormons! Third World appeals! Surveyors! I tell you something, it's never to your advantage.

Another ring on the doorbell

Sandra goes to the door

Norman takes up the remote control and plays "I've Got You Under My Skin". He sings with Frankie, closing his eyes tight, singing with all his heart, as if to keep out everything, as if nothing else existed

Sandra (*off: her voice from the street door at first showing surprise*) Oh, Mr de Groot. Please come in. I didn't expect ...

Sandra enters with Phillip de Groot. He is a charming, good-looking, open man who smiles a lot. His voice is soft and gentle. He always listens and never interrupts

Sandra turns Sinatra off. Norman, who has been moving around the room singing, oblivious, is suddenly marooned without the support of Mr Sinatra

Norman (*angrily*) Sandra! (*But his anger immediately subsides when he sees Phillip. He smiles*)
Phillip I do hope it's not inconvenient.

Norman scrutinizes Phillip

Sandra Not at all. Mr de Groot. This is my brother, Norman.
Phillip Ah yes. You're the antiquarian bookbinder.
Norman I'm not so old.

Laughter all round

Phillip I'm so pleased to meet you. (*He turns to Sandra*) Sandra, I brought this book for you. The one I was telling you about. It's *The Book of Change*.
Norman The *I Ching*.
Phillip Ah, I see I'm amongst people who know a thing or two. Who understand. How refreshing. (*To Sandra*) I thought you might be interested.
Sandra (*taking it*) How thoughtful, Mr de Groot! *The Book of Change*. Mmmm! If it can change me I'm more than interested.
Phillip I'm sure you are perfectly splendid as you are.
Sandra Thank you.
Phillip Look! I mustn't keep you——
Sandra No. Please stay. This book looks fascinating. Maybe you can explain it all to me.
Phillip With pleasure.
Sandra Would you like a cup of tea, Mr de Groot?
Phillip How kind of you. But please call me Phillip.
Norman Please, do sit down, Mr de Groot.

Phillip Thank you.
Sandra Phillip!
Phillip Thank you.
Sandra Lapsang Souchong? Or some Formosa Oolong? On the other hand, if you would like something a little more exotic we could possibly stretch to some Tetley's teabags.

Sandra and Phillip laugh. Norman wears a fixed smile

Phillip Whatever you decide is fine by me.

Sandra smiles and goes to the kitchen

Sandra Would you like a top-up, Norman?
Norman No thank you, Sandra. I'm a little pushed this morning. (*He goes back to his workbench*)

Pause

Phillip Tell me about bookbinding Norman?
Norman What? Here and now? It's an enormous subject.
Phillip I appreciate that. Give me the essence, what it actually means. I'm very interested.
Norman (*pleased*) Right! Hold this a moment. (*He plonks the book he has completed into Phillip's arms*) That's the truth.
Phillip Ah, you want the spirit of the book to enter me. I see. This is amazing. The smell, the weight. The spirit.
Norman Yeah. Thank God, it's off my hands tomorrow. It was an absolute cow. I think of all of them as individuals. Neighbours. Friends. Relatives. Ancestors. Children who must leave home.
Phillip Fascinating. Tell me about your work.
Norman The work is the work.
Phillip (*intensely*) I mean — what does it mean to you?
Norman The book is the person, right? Nerves, desires, blood. Dreams. It's the meaning of us. It's us. And the binding holds the book together. It's the outer skeleton. Without it we'd fall apart. Tell me about you and your work.
Phillip I am a seeker.
Sandra (*returning with tea*) Here you are.
Phillip Ah, how very kind. I used to be an architect. Not bad. Mainly hack work; the exigencies of modern life. The realities. The compromises one has to make. Then one day, whilst walking in China — I was walking along the Great Wall actually — I had a kind of mystical experience. It was, if you like, my Road to Damascus. An inner voice boomed. Phillip de Groot! What are you doing with your life? What was I doing indeed? From that moment on I was plagued with inner doubt. What is the meaning of me? What is the meaning of existence? Is there a meaning? Should there be a meaning? *Qui somme nous? Où allons nous?* The binding is the person, indeed. But my binding fell away. I was terrified. I almost fell apart.
Sandra In that case have a biscuit. (*She hands him a biscuit*)

Act I, Scene 2   15

Phillip Ginger nuts. How very nice. How did you know these were my favourites? Anyway, I survived that greatest crisis in my life. And I chucked it all in. I dabbled in many things, trying to find my new self. I've travelled extensively in India. Did voluntary work amongst the bereft of Africa. All the time questioning, surviving. You see me as I am, a seeker. I believe we are the stuff that dreams are made of but we, man, humankind, is in terrible danger. And we are the danger. I have a modest income. A legacy. I am content, yet not complacent. I am still searching for my true vocation. I hope that answers your question.
Sandra Oh yes. Absolutely.
Norman Thank you. Please excuse me.
Sandra Oh. Norman.
Norman Sorry. I've got so much to do. Packing. Letters to write. Phone calls. Nice to meet you, Mr de Groot.
Phillip Phillip. Please. And the pleasure's been all mine, Norman.
Sandra Oh dear, I thought perhaps we could all go to the Festival Hall or somewhere. The Courtauld Collection or the Tate Gallery.
Norman Excuse me. I'll take your coat. Make this room look a bit tidier. Shall I put it in your room, Sandra?
Sandra If you don't mind. What a darling.

Norman takes the things and goes to her room. The phone rings. Sandra seems apprehensive, answers it, talks quietly. Norman watches her

Yes? I can't talk about that now. Yes. Thank you. (*She hangs up and smiles*)
Norman Who was that? (*He searches through her pockets*)
Sandra No-one.

Norman finds a letter in her pocket. He immediately shoves it into his jacket and goes to his room

Norman Who was that?
Sandra Wrong number.

Norman lies on his bed and reads the letter. Whereupon he immediately covers himself with a blanket. He remains like that, still and silent, curled into himself, entirely covered over in a foetal position. His posture is a menacing counterpoint to the following scene

Phillip What a lovely house. What wonderful proportions. What high ceilings. One can think in this room.
Sandra I was born here. In this very room. It's a trap. All my life I've longed to get away.
Phillip Trapped. I don't understand. Why?
Sandra It's too big, too full of ghosts. Too full of my own laughter.
Phillip I don't understand.
Sandra I don't go upstairs. I'm afraid of my ghost. My childhood that roams around up there. She wants revenge. And can you blame her?
Phillip It's unoccupied?
Sandra Yes.

Phillip This huge house? Don't you let rooms?
Sandra Let rooms do what?

Laughter when the joke sinks in

We don't approve of strangers, Phillip! I'm worried about Norman. He never goes out.
Phillip Perhaps I can help. Please feel you can trust me.
Sandra Many, many thanks. You're very sweet. It's all right. It's nothing. Sometimes I get a little depressed.
Phillip Don't we all.
Sandra Tell me about *The Book of Change*.
Phillip Yes indeed. And later perhaps I'll tell your fortune.
Sandra Maybe. I'm not sure.
Phillip I think you're very nice. Very deep, very beautiful.
Sandra Me beautiful? Come on.
Phillip Deeply beautiful. Where it matters. Your eyes are so intelligent. They've seen it all, yet they avoid despair. They still dart, with expectancy.
Sandra Phillip. Talk about the *I Ching*, not about me.
Phillip Certainly. It's three thousand years old. It's one of the oldest books ever written. It is concerned with ways of attaining inner happiness rather than material success. It is not based on a religious doctrine, nor is it a divine revelation. It has not evolved from tribal law or folklore. Rather it is based on the observation of nature, of human life; the interaction of universal law, of free will, of destiny, individual behaviour. It does not emphasize the eternal; it is a book of ancient wisdom, recognizing that time is the essential factor in the structure of the world and in the development of the individual. You see, my dear Sandra, change itself gives meaning to life, gives stability, change itself is the only unchanging eternal in a world of transcendental reality.

As he speaks time has passed. The speech has been symbolic, as if he has talked for a long time. It is now time for him to go. They are at the door, she is handing him his coat

Sandra Many thanks for coming round and loaning me this book. I shall read it with great interest.
Phillip I am delighted. It was a pleasure meeting you and your brother. Sandra! I must see you again. And soon.
Sandra I hope so.
Phillip Perhaps the library tomorrow. Shall I telephone you?
Sandra That will be nice.
Phillip Please be honest. I do hope it's not inconvenient.
Sandra It will be very nice to hear from you.
Phillip You've made me very happy.
Sandra And you me.
Phillip I have a glow inside.
Sandra So do I. Goodbye Phillip.

Phillip goes

Act I, Scene 2

(*She smiles, looks at her reflection in the mirror, adopting several rather theatrical and sexy poses*) I'm Shanghai Lil. So take me, Phillip, take me to China. Take me anywhere. Take me. To Brighton, West Hampstead. Anywhere but Streatham. Enough of that crap, Sandra. Romance is dangerous. The other side of the coin is disaster. Mr de Groot is real. He has no white charger. He will not sweep you into his arms. No-one will come with the answer. He will not shatter you with passion. Grow up. This is what you really need. Get smart. You need a platonic lover; a gentle affinity. You need someone different. Someone not the usual beast. Who only wants to get into my knickers. Are you sure Sandra? Are you absolutely sure? Listen, I'm absolutely sure. This is the first man I've met for years and years who is really different. This is someone I could settle for, settle with. But give it time, Sandra. Don't rush things. Don't spoil things by being too hasty. Thank you, Sandra.

Norman has quietly entered, unnoticed by Sandra, and is watching her. He seems so sinister that we think almost anything could happen here

Everything comes to those who wait.

Norman goes towards her back, his hands raised forward in a strangling position. She suddenly turns

Norman!
Norman You can do with a massage.
Sandra I certainly can.

Norman starts to massage her neck

Norman Do you like him?
Sandra He's very nice.
Norman I liked him very much. You must invite him again.
Sandra I will. Oh Norman, your hands bring a warm pink light. What would I do without you?
Norman Sometimes though, I get afraid, Sandra.
Sandra I know darling, I'm here to help you.
Norman We love it here, don't we? This is the only place we want to be. Isn't that right, Sandra.
Sandra Yes. I love it here.
Norman (*as if recollecting a childhood ritual*) We must never leave. Never, never.
Sandra Never leave. Never, never.
Norman And you will never leave me here, will you? You will never try to sell this house?
Sandra Sell it? Leave you here? Of course not. What's got into you today?
Norman This, you lousy bitch. (*He grabs her hair*) This has got into me.
Sandra Norman! Norman! Please! What are you doing?
Norman This! This! You lump of shit with two eyes. (*He holds up the letter*)
Sandra Norman! How dare you go through my things!
Norman It fell from your pocket.
Sandra Liar! Liar!

Norman It fell! It fell!
Sandra I can explain! Everything!
Norman All right! Explain! And then I'll kill you. After all your promises; you contact an estate agent. Of all the lowest worms that ever crawled through slime. An estate agent!
Sandra Norman. I can explain.
Norman I'm dreaming this. You're trying to destroy me, (*He lets her go, sits with his head in his hands*)
Sandra I can explain.
Norman (*crying*) Treacherous cow!
Sandra I can explain everything.
Norman Why? Why?
Sandra Listen darling. Please listen. I never want to live anywhere else. I promised them. I swear on their memory. Please believe me?
Norman (*nodding*) Then why did you consult the entrails? Why did you write to Messrs Viscera and Co?
Sandra I was being practical for once in my life. I just wanted to find out the market value. Norman, we're people of substance who live in the shadows.
Norman So? We're not selling. You said so. So what's the point?
Sandra I just wanted to feel rich. Then I would feel more at ease if we indulged.
Norman In what?
Sandra We should go on a cruise, Norman. To get you out into the sunshine. You never, never go out. It's serious my love. But the sea is not the streets; you'll be safe there, with me. I wanted us to go to Knossos to explore the labyrinth. To sail on an Hellenic cruise, with an archeologist in attendance. To hear the horn of Ulysses blowing through a night of six trillion stars.
Norman I didn't know Ulysses had the horn. Sorry.
Sandra Men! You're all the same. Why are you all so vulgar? Be serious, Norman.
Norman Please forgive me. I should know better.
Sandra You know what I promised Daddy. You know I vowed to look after you and never let you out of my sight, and would always strive for your happiness. You know I've only ever thought of you.
Norman But you promised never to contact an estate agent. Remember? Only last week!
Sandra It was an impulse, out of love. Forgive me. I shall never do it again. We don't need to sell this house. Now or ever.
Norman And our voyage to Knossos?
Sandra Darling! We go whenever we like. We've got all that money in the Building Society. Remember? We're not exactly starving. So why not? Norman, why don't we? I'll phone a travel agent tomorrow.
Norman Yes. We'll go next winter. We'll cheat. And when we land in the lemon sunshine, first thing we'll buy *The Times*, and read all about the blizzards. And we'll laugh and drink retsina and break plates in cafes, applauded by smiling, toothless old men. Yes. We will go Sandra, next

Act I, Scene 2

year. We'll certainly go. I'm starving Sandra. If I don't eat immediately I shall expire. How about a fantastic meringue with cream? Can I create one for you?

Sandra Thanks. I feel rather full. (*Taking up the book Phillip gave her*) The *I Ching*. This is wonderful stuff.

Norman *The Book of Change*. If he lets you keep it I shall bind it for you.

Sandra Perfect.

Norman Sandra, you are the nicest person ever invented. And I am warped and wicked and don't deserve you. How could I believe such things? How could I believe you just wanted to destroy me and escape?

He goes to the kitchen, prepares his meringue. She goes to the radiogram, selects a record, plays it. Sinatra sings "High Hopes." Norman returns with the meringue and stands close, both of them standing over the revolving record. She is reading the "I Ching." He wants her to pay attention

Norman What was his first engagement after leaving Dorsey?

Sandra Was it The Paramount?

Norman It was The Paramount. But when was it? I want the exact date.

Sandra Sorry. I defer to the grand master.

Norman Sandra! It was at The Paramount! New York. December thirty-first. Nineteen forty-two. Who was playing there at the time?

Sandra No good. I'm rusty today.

Norman Benny Goodman. And what did Mr Goodman say? How did he introduce him?

Sandra "And now for the greatest——"

Norman No! No! At that time he'd never even heard of him. He just said "And now—Frank Sinatra."

Norman is eating and moving backwards and forwards in childlike autistic motion. Sandra reads her book

(*Quietly*) Sandra! If you double-cross me, we'll never survive.

Sandra looks at her brother. She smiles but is chilled. He smiles back and continues swaying. He turns up the volume until Sinatra's voice seems to drown everything

CURTAIN

ACT II

Scene 1

The same. Two weeks later. Sunday afternoon

The stage is empty, but there is a clattering of plates and cutlery in the kitchen cupboard. Then we hear Norman singing "Something's Gotta Give". He emerges from the cupboard with a birthday cake, beginning to sing "Happy Birthday to me". The phone rings. He answers it

Hallo! Tibetan Embassy! ... Sorry. Her Serene Imperial Majesty Queen Sandra Lewis the First is taking a walk over Streatham Common with her Prime Minister. Sorry. Just joking. Actually my sister is not here. Can I help? ... Who? ... Sullivan and Nash? Estate Agents? It's Sunday! Do you work today? ... How enterprising ... Are you really? I see ... Was she now? How very nice. One little problem however Miss?——Miss Coombes-Watson. I said my sister wasn't here. I should have said my sister wasn't all here. She resides in Banstead as a matter of fact. You know, the nut house. She has illusions. She believes she is a person of property, for which she is undergoing treatment. But they do let her out occasionally, and during that time she has an uncontrollable urge to phone up posh bitches like you. So fuck off and stop wasting my time. You tight-arsed little shit from the shires. (*He puts the phone down, laughs*) It's those you love who give you the problems. (*He goes to Sandra's room, wonders if there is any place he hasn't searched. He looks under her bed, then through a wardrobe, tries on one of her hats, looks at himself in the mirror, poses. Then he picks up the book on her small bedside table and takes it into the living room and starts to read*) "The Book of Change, when not in use, should be kept wrapped in clean silk or cloth, at an elevation not lower than the shoulders of a man standing erect——" (*he laughs*) Norman Lewis at your service! (*He laughs again*) "Something's gotta give, something's gotta give——" *The Book of Change*! Codswollop! You are what you are. You're lumbered! (*He cuts himself a slice of cake and starts to eat it*) Sandra won't mind. Mmmm!

He plays Sinatra on CD. A few lines from "Young At Heart" are heard then he turns off the music

Why not? I've been dependent on that bitch for too long. I'm going out. (*Pleased with himself he gets his coat and hat and scarf*) God! Dare I? (*His eyes close, as if praying*) Please God. (*Into the mirror*) You can do anything! Stand straight. Show her! Show the bitch. You can do anything. Confidence! That's all it takes. Here you go. Help! Nothing to it. What

Act II, Scene 1

you got to lose? Your life, that's all. It's a piece of cake. And it's my cake. (*He cuts another slice of cake and munches it*)

Gravely, with great determination, he strides out, slamming the door. For a moment we think he has succeeded but then he comes rushing back in again

Sod God! Anyway, nowhere to go. (*He takes off his hat and coat, puts Sinatra back on CD and whistles with the music while he continues working*) All her fault! Bitch!

Soon Sandra and Phillip enter. They are laughing

Norman smiles, happy to see them

Hallo darling?

But to his chagrin, Sandra turns off the music

Nice walk?

Sandra Very nice. Wasn't it, Phillip?

Phillip It was a perfect walk. Invigorating. Uplifting. Just the job for a Sunday afternoon.

Sandra We walked over the Common and watched the kids flying kites. Remember Norman, Mummy and Daddy taking us there when we were very young?

Norman Yes. Every Sunday.

Sandra You were so good at it. I couldn't get mine in the air. Let's have some tea?

Phillip What a good idea. Shall I make it?

Sandra No. You just sit down and take the weight off your brain. I won't be a moment. (*She goes to the kitchen cupboard and returns with an empty milk bottle, holding it up for Norman to see*)

Sandra Norman!

Norman It's still on the doorstep.

Sandra But you've been here all day.

She sighs, but then goes out to get the milk

Phillip, for a moment, considers broaching something possibly delicate

Phillip Norman, may I be frank with you?

Norman As long as you're Frank and not Frankie. (*He laughs raucously at his joke*) Shoot!

Phillip I know you may be worried.

Norman Oh? Why should I be worried?

Phillip I don't blame you if you are perhaps a little suspicious of me.

Norman Suspicious? My dear fellow, I don't know what you're talking about.

Phillip I just want to say this. Please, rest assured that I have nothing but the highest respect and regard for you and your sister. I feel very close to both of you. Consider me as someone you can turn to.

Norman Phillip, that's very nice.

Phillip Thank you. (*He hears Sandra about to return. Softly, confidentially*) I'm so pleased we've had this chat.

Sandra returns and starts to get some tea

(*Seeing the cake*) What a splendid cake.
Norman It's my birthday cake. Would you like some?
Phillip Yes please. If that's all right.

Norman cuts Phillip a wedge

Sandra What! What are you doing?
Phillip I'm so sorry.
Sandra Oh dear. You may as well eat it now. Norman! Why? You've spoiled everything. Your birthday is the day after tomorrow! It looks so pathetic now. What am I going to do with you?
Norman I was suddenly starving. I'm sorry.
Phillip Are you having a party? Am I invited?
Sandra That's up to Norman.
Norman I'll have to think about it. Tell me more about kite flying, Phillip.
Phillip I say! That's a good idea! Why don't we go kite flying together, Norman.
Sandra Yes! (*Suddenly there is light at the end of a tunnel. If Norman gets out her problems decrease*) Why don't you?
Norman (*sudden angst and anger*) No. Just tell me about it.
Phillip (*sensing the undercurrents*) Oh. Yes! Kite flying has an amazing history. They're called kites after the bird. In German of course it is *Drache*, dragon. It's fascinating.
Sandra (*making tea. Not really interested*) Yes.
Phillip Kites were invented by Archytas of Tarentum, four centuries before Jesus Christ, the magician.
Norman Fascinating. He's so brilliant Sandra. He has all this amazing knowledge stored in his brain.
Phillip Exactly. You've hit it on the head.
Norman (*mumbling murderously*) If only I could.
Phillip (*misinterpreting*) You can. Anyone can. The brain is merely a super computer.
Norman Sandra! I've written you a new poem.
Phillip You write poetry? Please! I'd love to hear it.
Sandra Another in your microwave series?

Norman nods

Shoot.
Norman This poem is dedicated to my sister, Sandra Lewis. It's called "Pussy in a microwave" (*He reads the poem*) "Meee———OWW!" Like it? Phillip?
Phillip It's—let me—see. It's extremely sardonic, isn't it.
Norman Do you understand it?
Sandra Norman!
Phillip Yes, I think I do understand it. It's saying a lot. Less is more.

Act II, Scene 1

Norman Oh! Wonderful! This is music to my ears.
Sandra Phillip, don't be taken in. Norman's being his usual naughty little self.
Norman Sandra!
Phillip Sandra! I really do feel the poem has some significance. There is more in this poem than meets the mouth. I detect an underlying existential cosmic cruelty.
Norman That's really funny. You are a real comic. You're not really as serious as you seem.
Phillip You've twigged me, my friend.

Sandra is happy that the two men seem to be hitting it off

But would you say I got your poem right?
Norman I would say you have understood it. Precisely.
Phillip Thank you.
Norman Bring him here often, Sandra. He's good for me. We might unearth my ego.
Phillip What do you think, Sandra?
Sandra I think my brother is very, very wicked. And I am dying of thirst.

She goes and kisses Norman. He seems far away

Anyone at home? Sometimes he inhabits dark, far away places. Norman! What's going on in that horrid little brain?
Norman Sorry! So sorry. I was miles away.
Phillip Yes. It would be nice to take up kite flying. A Korean general once inspired his troops by sending up a kite with a lantern attached. It was taken by his army as a new star, a divine omen of victory.
Norman (*yawning*) If you will excuse me. (*He looks at his watch*) Time for my nap.
Sandra I poured you tea.
Norman Thank you Sandra. But I must go to the Land of Kites. I go there every day at this time. Who knows, I may meet your Korean general today. Thank you for the cup of tea. I shall warm it up later in the microwave. Phillip. It's all been very interesting. Thank you so much for sharing my birthday cake. (*He kisses Sandra, sees that Phillip has not yet touched his slice of cake*) Well, eat it Phillip.
Phillip Thank you very much. I'm savouring this.
Sandra Mmmmm! Sleep well Norm.

Norman, singing a snatch of "Something's Gotta Give", goes to his room. He lies on the bed, covers himself with a padded quilt, closes his eyes, seems to sleep immediately

Phillip (*nibbling at his cake*) We're getting on very well, aren't we.
Sandra I hope so. Who knows what goes on in that brain.
Phillip He's absolutely original.
Sandra He's an absolute monster.

Phillip goes over to the radiogram and inspects the record collection

Phillip You must have every record Ol' Blue Eyes ever recorded.
Sandra Just about.
Phillip I love this one. May I play it?
Sandra Need you ask.

Phillip puts the record on. Sinatra sings "You Make Me Feel So Young"

Beautiful. Often I lose all my faith. Mr Sinatra restores it at once with a song. (*She sits down with her tea, sits back, muses*) Music takes you back. My parents loved him.
Phillip Who? Sinatra?
Sandra No. Norman. They hated Sinatra. They hated anything that wasn't Grand Opera. Norman was grand opera from the moment he was born. He's very fond of you, you know.
Phillip That delights me. He is a person of originality, of real integrity.
Sandra I'm really surprised. Normally he doesn't take to strangers.
Phillip I'm gratified. But I never felt I was a stranger. Why did you never fall in love Sandra?
Sandra My brother needed me. Please take the record off.

Phillip seems mildly surprised

Sometimes Mr Sinatra makes me too emotional.

He stops the music

Tell me some more about *The Book of Change*.
Phillip Right. You see, the authors of the *I Ching* did not regard the future as unalterable. They thought in terms of mighty sequences of change, like the process of the four seasons. A river, now gushing through a narrow gorge, now fighting its way through rocky shallows, now running smoothly and slowly, destined sooner or later to reach the sea.
Sandra I remember the seashore. Blankenberg. We always went there. Me paddling, splashing my father, giggling, dressed all in white. The sun! Shattered gold, dazzling bright. "Daddy! Daddy! Please! More flying angels! Throw me up high into the sky! Ever so high. Don't ever stop!" Sorry Phillip. I interrupted.
Phillip That's all right. You carry on.
Sandra Certain moments are indelible; they are fused in the brain. They float up from the dark. I shall never forget the monster, that incredible moment when he smiles and gently plays with the child.
Phillip I don't——I don't know what you're talking about.
Sandra Frankenstein! Didn't you see the film? It haunts me.
Phillip No. (*Intensely*) Please tell me about it.
Sandra It's memorable. Unforgettable. The moster is being chased. He has done terrible things; he is capable of monstrous acts. Not his fault. That's his nature.
Phillip Ah yes! In Milton's *Paradise Lost* there is this great dilemma; God creates Satan. Surely therefore Satan has a role to play in the divine purpose, in the mystery of existence. Similarly with Iscariot. Why is he not called Saint Judas?

Act II, Scene 1

Sandra Phillip! I was describing a golden moment from my past!
Phillip I'm sorry. I do get carried away. Do shoot me down whenever you feel the need.
Sandra So there he is in the forest, the monster, running for his life, this potent, powerful creature. When he comes across a beautiful little girl with golden hair, on a swing, singing to herself. He stops, smiles and strokes her hair. She smiles up at him. Time stops. It is a moment of absolute beauty. Then he rushes on, soon to be destroyed.
Phillip "—what rough beast, its hour come round at last, slouches towards Bethlehem to be born". Sandra, many, many thanks for a glorious day. I hope I haven't overstayed my welcome.
Sandra No. Never. Indeed, must you go now?
Phillip (*consulting his watch*) Unfortunately. I have a cello lesson in half an hour.
Sandra Oh, I didn't know you played the cello.
Phillip I wouldn't exactly call what I do playing. I'm a mere novice.
Sandra I'd love to hear you sometime.
Phillip That would be very nice. Meanwhile I shall pick you up at——is seven thirty all right?
Sandra Yes.

Sandra smiles, the moment is highly charged with possibilities. They stand close as if to embrace, but Phillip avoids getting closer

Phillip I've booked a table. I hope you like Thai food?
Sandra I've never had it.
Phillip You'll love it. Everything comes to those who wait.
Sandra I hope so.
Phillip Marvellous. See you later.

He goes

Sandra Thank you, Phillip. Thank you. (*She closes the door, but when she turns round . . .*)

Norman is there, arms outstretched coming towards her, lumbering like an imbecilic monster

My God! The monster emerges.

Now we think it is possible that Norman overheard the conversation between Sandra and Phillip

Norman I am yours to command, Mistress Frankenstein. Did I scare you?
Sandra Not more than usual. Were you listening just now?
Norman Listening? What are you talking about?
Sandra How did you know Phillip and I were talking about Frankenstein just before he left?
Norman How did you greet me when I came in?
Sandra I forget.
Norman You said "The monster emerges." So naturally I talk about Frankenstein.

Sandra Did I? Oh yes, maybe I did. Hold on. Didn't you have your arms outstretched, just like the monster, before I even mentioned him. Oh dear, I'm totally confused. I'm sorry. I always seem to get at you. I must remember to be nicer.

Norman I forgive you. I mean, Frankenstein is an eternal myth. It's the greatest myth. But it's true. It's man stealing fire from the gods. It's man over-reaching. I hope Phillip isn't overreaching.

Sandra In which way?

Norman Getting too close.

Sandra Phillip is very nice and very respectful. And absolutely decent. So don't you dare insinuate anything and shut up.

Norman Sandra! Sweetheart! Now it's my turn to apologize. I like Phillip. I think he is a very nice man. But you can understand I don't relish the idea of anyone entering our lives. (*He picks up the "I Ching", and reads at random*) "Righteous persistance brings good fortune." Ha! Crap! We are where we are. There's no way out. We're well and truly trapped. Thank God.

Sandra Have you been rummaging through my room again?

Norman How dare you! How dare you! Would I do a thing like that?

Sandra Yes! I left this book beside my bed. How did it get in here?

Norman (*reading*) "The wild goose moves gradually towards the hillock." (*He laughs, hands her the book*)

Sandra (*jokingly hitting him on the head with the book*) Hate you!

Norman You're lovely. Hey! Guess what? Guess what we have got for dinner tonight? Gigot of English lamb. Perfecto! With new potatoes. Mint sauce. And mange tout. Remember you got it from Marks last Friday.

Sandra Did I?

Norman Isn't it wonderful. We are the Microwave Chilled Food generation. But how did we and mankind manage before it? Please invite Philip for dinner . . .

Sandra Darling! I'm so sorry. Phillip is taking me to a restaurant this evening.

Norman Oh. That's nice.

Sandra Norman! Please believe me. Nothing will change between us. Whatever happens.

Norman Sandra, what you do is up to you. It's your life.

She goes to her room. He goes to the radiogram, looking through the records

Sandra!

Sandra Yes, darling?

Norman No. Nothing.

Sandra Come on. What were you going to say?

Norman It's just—sometimes I ask myself. What is he after? What does he really want?

Norman puts on a record, "Come Fly With Me", then grabs her, dances with her. She seems chilled, lifeless, automatic, as he smiles and swirls her around

CURTAIN

Act II, Scene 2   27

                                    SCENE 2

Later that night

Mahler plays on the radiogram

Norman is slumped into an armchair, far away, staring into infinite space. There is a feeling of total resignation. But he suddenly sits up, looks at his watch, jumps up and quickly paces the room as if he were a caged animal. Then he gets an idea. He goes to his room, pulls back his bedclothes, and, using pillows, he quickly improvises a human effigy, he covers this over, and stands back to inspect his handiwork

Singing "Something's Gotta Give" Norman rubs his hands and leaves his room. He removes the Mahler and puts Sinatra on the CD player. Sinatra sings, "All The Way". He hears noise outside, quickly switches off the CD then he looks around and quickly hides within the kitchen cupboard. There is silence

Sandra and Phillip enter. They stand close, look at each other intently, but do not speak

Sandra goes to Norman's room, quietly opens the door, sees the sleeping figure, seems pleased, returns to Phillip

Sandra He's flat out. The sleep of the just. Just like a baby. I love him. If I could get away it might be the making of him. But he's so dependent on me. (*There is a pause as a new thought occurs to her*) Perhaps I've become too dependent on that dependence. If only I could escape.
Phillip No. You don't really want to do that. This place is so perfect. (*he takes up the remote control and switches on the music*)

Sinatra sings "All the Way"

   Please dance with me.

She smiles but seems uneasy

   Come on.

Almost reluctantly she moves towards him. He holds her, but not too close. They slowly dance

Sandra Norman has invited you to his party.
Phillip That's very nice of him.
Sandra He really wants you to come.
Phillip Good. Lots of others coming?
Sandra No. There'll just be the three of us.
Phillip Oh! (*He covers his surprise*) What shall I get him for a present. The *Iliad* of Homer?
Sandra He'd love some Belgian chocolates.
Phillip *Mui Bien!* Shall be done. *Excellente!*

They continue dancing

Sandra, what would he do without you?
Sandra I cannot even think of that possibility.
Phillip Why did you never marry?
Sandra Nobody ever asked me. Nobody that I wanted. Anyway, I'm no catch.
Phillip That's ridiculous.
Sandra My brother needs me.
Phillip And what do you need?
Sandra I don't like this sort of talk.
Phillip Sorry. So what are your immediate plans?
Sandra Plans? I just want to be shot of this place.
Phillip (*with real consternation*) What? Sandra! Most people would sell their soul to own a big beautiful house like this. You cannot even consider giving it all up.
Sandra Phillip, can I trust you?
Phillip Sandra! (*His exclamation is meant to say everything*)
Sandra It's wonderful to be able to actually talk to someone. In many ways Norman is perfectly normal but sometimes he has such terrible, murderous tantrums. I can't tell you how awful it is.
Phillip Sandra, I do feel for you. For him. Have you sought help?
Sandra Time and again. At the moment he's not too bad. He's happy. Doctor Sinatra is the very best therapy. He helps us enormously. My recurring dream is to get away.
Phillip I think your life is about to change. But the change is happening within you. This house is your rock. Your real security. You can find true happiness here. You must dismiss all thoughts of selling it, of running away. The fact is you cannot run away from yourself.

They stop dancing

Sandra Phillip, what is the answer? For me.
Phillip The answer is in yourself. And you must promise that you will make no decisions and do nothing foolish without consulting me?
Sandra I promise.
Phillip Good. I'm sure we can find ways of making your life and all this beautiful.
Sandra You make everything sound so possible. So positive. Tell me more about yourself.
Phillip Now? Are you interested?
Sandra Absolutely. Do you know Norman was only saying earlier, we really know nothing about Phillip.
Phillip Nothing much to know.
Sandra Please tell me everything.
Phillip Everything was emptiness; endless, boring Basingstoke. "Phillip! Please take off your muddy shoes; wash your paws, you mucky pup. Finished? Then place your knife and fork together. Shush! Don't raise your voice." But deep down they were covering up. They were common. They hated everything, everyone so much. They died quietly, the way they lived. After that I drifted and I have drifted ever since. I'm so tired of

Act II, Scene 2

drifting. This is paradise. The clutter. Soon as I saw you I wanted to get in, to join you, to belong.

Sandra Shall we have some tea?

Phillip I've dabbled in many things, to earn a living, but recently I've been searching for an alternative way of living on this earth. I also feel the need to settle down. My thoughts are crystalizing. I'm thinking of doing something; something useful, spiritually. Something specific; a small, pleasant, morally uplifting venture. But I need a partner. One does in life.

Sandra Oh?

Phillip One needs to externalize. To prove one has lived; and to some purpose.

Sandra What is this idea you have? Sounds fascinating.

Phillip Sandra, do you realize that you have changed my life. And now we need to talk about us.

Sandra Please Phillip. Not now. Not yet. Tell me about your business idea.

Phillip The world is starved of new ways of doing things. I want to open a place where we can apply the esoteric wisdom of the ages, where we can help solve the desperate tensions of the modern world.

Sandra *We?*

Phillip I need a partner. Dance with me. (*He puts on a CD*)

Sinatra sings "Something's Gotta Give". She slowly dances towards him. They dance

Sandra, you know what's happening.

Sandra Yes. I mustn't let it.

Phillip I've fallen in love with you. You feel the same.

Sandra It's too soon. Too soon. We're going too fast.

They stand still, they are close, touching, just staring at each other

No! Please don't. (*She breaks away*)

But Phillip goes to her and she turns around, as if realizing she now cannot avoid the inevitable. He kisses her. At first she is stiff but soon she responds. They kiss again. Then they stand silently, as if ready for an affray of passion. Suddenly Norman chuckles. Sandra goes quickly to the kitchen cupboard

Norman is revealed, crouching there, smiling

You monster!

Norman emerges. As he goes towards his room, his smile is fixed

Norman (*quietly*) You've ruined my life. (*He enters his room and locks the door*)

Sandra You'd better go.

Phillip gets his things and goes to the door

Phillip I'm so sorry. Will you be all right?

Sandra Yes. I can handle this.

Phillip Shall I see you tomorrow?

Sandra Phone me at work.
Phillip Goodnight.

Phillip exits

Sandra Goodnight. (*She closes the door then goes to Norman's room, knocks gently on the door*) Norman. Listen! I can explain everything. Please open the door.
Norman How dare you! How dare you discuss me with a stranger. How dare you! How dare you! How dare you! How dare you!
Sandra (*quietly cooing*) Norman, darling. Please open the door.
Norman Go away. You've ruined my life.
Sandra Everything's all right, darling. Norman! I need love. I love him.

Norman laughs quietly

I'm so happy. Don't you see. Life hasn't passed me by, after all. I'm so happy. I'm so happy. (*She bursts out crying*) It's so good for all of us. We're all going to be so happy. Norman!
Norman Go to hell!
Sandra I'm there already. (*She goes to her room*)

They both lie on their beds. The Lights go out. Dogs bark. The telephone rings three times. Norman sings in the dark "Something's Gotta Give". Distorted children's voices sing "Happy Birthday", as if from far away, perhaps in Norman's memory

Time passes. A few days later

The place is empty. No sign of either of them. The room seems in modest festive mood. A few balloons hang from the mantelpiece. The words "Happy Birthday Norman" are written on the mirror and the table is laid for a party

Sandra and Norman enter, their arms full of shopping

Norman Careful with the trifle. (*He dumps his things on the table, sits down in the armchair, closes his eyes and tries some deep breathing*)

Sandra unpacks, placing more goodies on the table—delicatessen, lemonade, cakes, etc

Well! I actually left the house. Dada!! (*He pretends to blow a trumpet*)
Sandra I'm so proud. You did it.
Norman Yes. I'm trying.
Sandra Very, very trying. But I'm so proud of you. It wasn't too bad, was it?
Norman No. It wasn't bad. It was terrible. Bridge is boring.
Sandra You were wonderful at the club. Debonaire, funny. You played brilliantly. Mrs Swift said "Sandra, your brother is so attractive, so charming, so good looking. Where have you been keeping him?". Mrs Swift was that most attractive and voracious widow I introduced you to, remember?
Norman No. I was concentrating. Holding on for dear life.

Act II, Scene 2

Sandra Anyway, you did it. It proves you can do it again. You're free. We can start living again. We're not trapped.
Norman We're all trapped. Between dark and dark. Hole and hole. I am never going out again. Sorry.
Sandra Well, I'm not trapped. I mean it. I'm getting out.
Norman Sandra! I just don't like the streets and I do not particularly care for the company of the human race. Please don't be cross with me. It's my birthday, remember? Please play Sinatra.

She goes to the radiogram and puts on Sinatra singing "Come Fly With Me"

Sandra Yes. Let's enjoy ourselves today. We'll have a wonderful time; all three of us. He's late. Hold on! Clean forgot. Your present!
Norman (*very excited*) It's something really special. I can tell.
Sandra How did you guess? Something really special. Close your eyes. Don't cheat.

He clenches his eyes overtight whilst she goes to her bedroom where she reaches under her bed and brings out a package

I do hope you like it. (*She places the package before him*) It's very special, very idiosyncratic. Open your eyes!
Norman (*opening his eyes*) Sandra! What is it? Can't wait. (*He tears off the wrapping. His eyes light up as he holds his present. It is a stuffed owl*) An owl. Sandra—An owl! What could be better? You know how much I love owls. It's beautiful. It's perfect. It's stuffed. It can't die. Welcome! Minerva! Wisdom is mine forever.
Sandra Sure you like it?
Norman It's the best present I ever had.
Sandra I found it by chance in a little junk shop in Marylebone Lane. Are you sure you like it?
Norman Sandra! I love it. I love it so much, I could eat it, stuffing and all. You are the most fantastic sister in the whole wide world. Give us a big kiss.

They hug and kiss and sway as Sinatra sings, but she struggles to get free

Sandra Norman! I can't breathe. You're holding me too tight.
Norman Sorry!

He releases her with a kiss. She turns off the music

Sandra darling, let's start the party now. Please.
Sandra We have to wait for Phillip.
Norman We have to wait for no-one. That trifle looks too inviting. (*He sits down, puts on a paper hat, smiles, leans across and puts one on her head*) Let's start, please. I love just the two of us. (*He starts to sing "Happy Birthday"*) Sandra, I don't want people. I have no vacancies. I am all full up with people. Take some trifle. Don't wanna wait.
Sandra He'll be here any minute now.
Norman Sandra, I don't think he'll be coming.
Sandra What are you talking about?

Norman (*ending his song*) Happy birthday to me. Who is this Phillip? Where did he come from? We know nothing about him.
Sandra Read your card. (*She takes a card from her handbag and gives it to him. Then she continues to search through her handbag*)
Norman (*singing to tune "Who Is Sylvia"*) "Who is Phillip? What is he? He comes from outer darkness——". Sorry. If he were the good King Arthur I would fear him. I fear any stranger except Mr Frank Sinatra, but then, he's no stranger.
Sandra Norman! (*still rummaging through her bag*) Norman! Where's my——where the hell is my Building Society account book? Norman! Where is my book?

He smiles, hands it to her

What! How dare you! How dare you take that from my bag. How dare you steal it from me. That book is mine. Mine. My personal property. That money is in my account. It is mine. My own personal savings.
Norman (*quietly*) Sandra! Five thousand pounds withdrawn? Yesterday? Look! This is an entry in your own little Building Society book. There! Five thousand pounds withdrawn.
Sandra How dare you! That is none of your business. I'm going out!
Norman No, you're not. You're staying here. (*He bars the door*)
Sandra I'll call Dr Sinclair.
Norman There's the telephone. Call her.

Sandra rushes to the phone, lifts the receiver, puts it down again

What have you done with the money? Or did Minerva cost that much? Has your love for me gone completely overboard? (*Now heavy*) WHAT HAVE YOU DONE WITH THE MONEY? (*He holds her wrists, is hurting her*) Tell me or I swear I'll murder you. What have you done with that money?
Sandra It's my money! It's my business. How dare you go through my things. I hate you. Hate you!
Norman Darling! Please! (*He tries to cuddle her*)
Sandra (*pushing him away*) Don't! Leave me alone. Don't you ever, ever pry into my personal affairs again. Understand?
Norman Sandra, you and I—We don't have a separate existence. If we are not us, who are we then? What have all the years meant? Nothing? Am I nothing? I feel so sorry for you.
Sandra (*laughing, ridiculing*) You? You feel sorry for me?
Norman (*letting her go*) What does that mean? Tell me. What does that mean.
Sandra It means nothing. Absolutely nothing. You've hurt me. Hurt me. (*She rubs her wrists*)
Norman Please forgive me. (*He tries kissing her wrists*) I don't mean to hurt you.

She pulls away

Bitch! I've suffered long enough because of you.

Act II, Scene 2

Sandra You've suffered? That's a joke.

Norman I've had enough. Think I need you? All my life you've used me as an excuse for your own fears, because you think you're as ugly as a turd. But now you've gone too far.

Sandra I've gone too far? (*She laughs*) That's it! Right! Why should I be afraid of you? I shall tell you what I've done with that money. I've done something sensible for the first time in my life.

Norman Not interested. Sorry Sandra. Argument over. Let's be friends. (*He goes to the table, eats voraciously*) Try some of these cakes. They're absolutely scrumptious. Mmmmm! Sandra, I'm saying this in the nicest possible way, in a spirit of conciliation. You fell for the oldest trick in the book. You of all people. You fell for a pathetic common con-man, didn't you? You just gave him that money. Admit! Admit! Anyway, it's not really your fault. That's the whole point about con-men; they're so believable.

Sandra Norman, he is not a con-man. Please listen. It's a partnership. We're going into business. For once in my life I'm striking out, I'm doing the right thing. I never told you any of this because I know how suspicious you are. But please believe me. I know exactly what I am doing.

Norman Let's face it, you fell for that superficial innocent charm. I'm not blaming you. I mean you are the most suspicious person in this world. If he can take you in he must be a genius. *The Book of Change* certainly changed you.

Sandra Norman! Phillip is a seer. A seeker. We are going to open an alternative meditation centre. It's all planned. It can't fail. It can't fail. God knows people need it. We're moving into a new age. We're going to have a fifty-fifty partnership. At last I can give up my terrible job, my bloody bondage. Phillip's arranging everything.

Norman Don't be ridiculous.

Sandra I love him. He loves me.

Norman The shortest short story in the world. Once upon a time they all lived happy ever after. So, the little lady suddenly believes in love, does she? Love is a squelch between sheets.

Sandra You filthy beast. What do you know of love? He's never touched me; he respects me; has never laid one finger on my body. He really loves me. And I really love him.

Norman Love! (*He laughs*) That's the funniest thing I heard. This is love. (*He takes the remote control and plays Sinatra*) Only this is love.

Sinatra sings "Young At Heart"

Sandra, I'm thinking only of you. Believe me. You slaved for years to save that money, and then you chucked it all away without a blink. Mind you it's worth it, if it gets that toad out of our lives.

Sandra Norman. He is not out of our lives. He's coming. He won't let me down.

Norman Sandra, accept that you'll never see him again.

They sit back in silence. There is a long pause and then there is a ring on the bell

Sandra (*smugly*) You think in clichés. (*She goes towards the door*) What do you know of people?
Norman (*suddenly taking over, sure of himself*) No! I'll go.
Sandra (*suddenly pleading, retreating*) But I must talk to him.
Norman SANDRA! I'm handling this.
Sandra We love each other that's all that matters.

The doorbell rings again

If you scare him away . . . ! (*She turns Sinatra off*) You're not giving him a chance. Norman, if you love me you will be very calm.
Norman Sandra! I cannot let anything, anything come between us.

The bell rings again

Or . . . do you want me to lose myself again?
Sandra No. No. (*Scared, seeing danger signs, she tries to calm him*) All right Norman, I'm trusting you. I'm leaving everything to you. I'm in your hands.
Norman Good. Because if I lose myself you know where that leads. So, I'm handling this. Right?
Sandra Yes, Norman! Whatever you say.
Norman (*calming suddenly, smiling*) Thank you. Thank you.

Norman goes to open the door, returning with Phillip

Good afternoon Phillip.
Phillip Happy birthday, Norman. I brought you some chocolates.
Norman How did you know I love them? I live for them. Amongst other things. (*He opens the packet*) Yum! All for me? Goodie, goodie, gumdrops. We almost started the party without you. Sorry.

He offers the chocolates but they refuse. He starts eating them voraciously

Oh! forgot! Your party hat. (*He places a paper hat on Phillip's head*)
Phillip How kind of you. Hallo Sandra.
Sandra Hallo Phillip.
Phillip Sandra! My, you look sad. Like a Modigliani. "*La Princessa esta trieste, que tendre la Princessa . . . ?*"
Sandra Thank you.
Norman Phillip! I too have something to quote. A new poem I've written in honour of the occasion.
Phillip Another in your microwave series?
Norman Yes. It's called "Viper in a Microwave." Here goes. 'Viper in a Microwave" And here's the poem. "Sssssssssssssssuss!!"

The laughter is forced

Phillip Wonderful. Such wit. Such élan. You ought to try and get them published.

Act II, Scene 2

Norman Thank you Phillip. And now I have something private to discuss with you. Sandra, would you leave us, please.
Phillip I want her to stay. I have something rather important—Sandra!
Sandra Please Phillip. Talk to Norman. (*She tries to signal to Phillip that the situation is quite critical*)

Norman opens Sandra's bedroom door, but she goes to the street door

Anyway, my eyes are hurting. I need to go to the chemist. (*Quietly to Norman*) Norman! Please be nice.
Norman I'm always nice.

Sandra puts on her coat

It's all right, Sandra. (*He opens the door*) Trust me.
Sandra Yeah! (*Serious*) Norman darling, please don't spoil things for me.

Sandra goes

Norman closes the door

Norman (*turning to face Phillip, hooting*) Hoohoo! You do look so funny in your hat. (*In this scene he will talk softly and gently, smiling all the time*)
Phillip I think I know what this is all about.
Norman Do you really?
Phillip Look, before you go any further I would just like to say something.
Norman Fine. Carry on.
Phillip Look! I know I must seem like a threat. You must loathe my guts for entering your life. I don't blame you. You see, I understand you. I know what you're going through.
Norman Oh? Phillip! Please continue.

For a moment we believe that Phillip is finding a real way into Norman's trust

Phillip When my mother died I, too, went to pieces. I was so deeply involved and in love with her. I was destroyed. I've been there Norman, I've been where you are. I know what you're going through. Please trust me.

We and Phillip believe now that Norman has been won over

Say something. I'm listening.
Norman (*gorging chocolates*) These are really good. Very special. Belgian chocolates. It was extremely thoughtful of you, Phillip.
Phillip Look! I don't like this playing.
Norman Said the spider to the fly. Trouble is I'm too fly.
Phillip Look! I don't have to——
Norman Phillip, my old china, I believe my sister has given you some money.
Phillip I can explain.
Norman Five thousand pounds to be exact. Not an enormous sum to John Paul Getty Junior I would think. What should Mr Sinatra offer at a time

like this? Let me see. Ah! He's singing this just for us. (*He switches on the CD*)

Sinatra is heard singing "Fools Rush In"

He knows. Frank is god. He is privy to all our human imperfections. He's far nicer than me. He never stands in judgment. (*He turns off the song*)

Phillip Listen! That money—it was a loan. You must believe me. You must give me a chance. OK, I'm not a conventional sort of chap, and I'll be perfectly honest I've knocked around, even been on the skids. I just—I just want to play fair and square with you. Because Sandra has changed my life.

All the while Norman smiles and eats chocolates

It just happened. I never believed it could. It was a tremendous stroke of luck, but in this life you have to grab when you get that chance. It comes only once in a lifetime. Just give me a chance. Norman, it's all fixed. Sandra and I are going to be full partners.

Norman Generous. Have your solicitors drawn up a contract?
Phillip That's all in the process, I can assure you.
Norman Marvellous.
Phillip I am going to devote all my life and energy to making this business a success. But please understand, Nothing need change. We can work from here. I have no intention of carrying her off.
Norman Oh, that's such a relief.
Phillip And we can live right here, all three of us. I just love this house. But the real truth is—I love her and I want to share my life with her, with both of you.
Norman That's beautiful Phillip.
Phillip Thank you.
Norman What have you done with the five thousand pounds?
Phillip Oh—that's lodged with my solicitors, of course.
Norman Of course. Would you like some birthday cake?
Phillip I would love some.

Norman cuts a huge slice of chocolate cake

Norman Here! Put that in your cake hole.

Phillip smiles with pleasure but Norman suddenly lunges towards him, pushing the cake into Phillip's mouth, and wiping it all over his face with his hand. Meanwhile Norman's other hand grips Phillip's arm, pushing it hard upward, twisting it behind his back. Now Norman punches Phillip, hard in the stomach, sending him flying to the ground, shocked, bewildered, spluttering cake, his eyes bulging with fear

Phillip HELP!
Norman (*still smiling as he smooths cake all over Phillip's face*) You're very good looking Phillip. You have such gentle, such beautiful eyes. You always smell so nice. I don't wish you real harm; not mutilation. I have no intention of hitting you over the skull with an iron bar. Unlike my sister,

Act II, Scene 2

Phillip, I have my head screwed on, even if it is screwed on the wrong way. (*But now he wipes away his smiling mask*) Listen! Craphound! How could you take advantage of a vulnerable, trusting woman?

Phillip has nothing to say. He can hardly make a sound with Norman's hands clasped across his mouth

Listen carefully. I am giving you exactly five minutes to say goodbye. Otherwise I am going to break both your legs. Is that understood?

Phillip nods

Smashing.

He releases Phillip, who sits down, quite shattered. Norman presses the remote control. The CD continues singing "Fools Rush In"

Sandra enters slowly

Phillip stands, dusts himself off, smiles

Sandra Hello boys. (*She turns the music off*)
Norman Phillip was just leaving. Weren't you, Phillip?

Phillip nods, uncertainly

Sandra Norman! Please! I must talk to Phillip.
Norman With pleasure. Goodbye Phillip. (*He goes to his room, sits on his bed*)
Phillip I have to go now, but I still feel the same about you.
Sandra I see.
Phillip Look. Your brother's not normal. But it makes no difference.
Sandra I see.
Phillip Why do you keep saying "I see"?
Sandra Phillip, I've been thinking.
Phillip Dreadful disease. We'll soon cure you of that.
Sandra Sometimes you suddenly see things, clearly. The scales fall from your eyes.
Phillip Yes. Sandra——(*Going towards her*)
Sandra You think—How did it happen? You realise you've been an idiot. But then you want to be proved wrong. (*Moving slowly backwards*) Phillip, please tell me I'm wrong.
Phillip You're wrong. (*He looks at his watch*) Tell you what! Let's meet later. Café Continental. Along the High Road. Two hours?
Sandra The five thousand? Where is it?
Phillip My solicitors. Where else?
Sandra May I phone them?
Phillip Of course.
Sandra What's the number?
Phillip Yes. The number. I've forgotten it, Sandra.
Sandra Of course.
Phillip Let me explain the facts, Sandra.

Sandra Yes, Phillip. What are the facts? How is your house in Brighton, Phillip? What about your pied-à-terre in West Hampstead, Phillip? You never took me there, Phillip.

Phillip I've tried Sandra. I really have. I don't want you to think that I didn't try, that I didn't care for you. Somehow. That's the truth. If you believe in that sort of thing. The fact is when I met you I was on my uppers.

Sandra Where is that five thousand?

Phillip Sandra, believe me, if I had it I'd return it to you. Fact is, I'm flat broke. Isn't that fantastic? That amount of money. Gone, just like that. A debt, you understand. Imperative to pay back. Very, very nasty uncaring people. At least you got me out of trouble. You saved my life, probably. So thank you. (*He looks at his watch*) So I suppose we won't be meeting in two hours. Must go. I promised Norman and a promise is a promise. (*He opens the door*)

Sandra Phillip, I would like to thank you.

Phillip What do you mean?

Sandra You won't understand, but you've opened the door for me. I'm getting out.

Phillip Sandra, don't kid yourself. You'll never get out.

Sandra Thank you, Phillip. Please go.

Phillip You have a great capacity for love. Too bad it's wasted. You're hungry. You're famished. You need sex; incessant sex. I could have given it to you, Sandra. I could have shown you what life's really all about. And you would have begged me, begged me for more. More! You need it, Sandra. You need it bad.

Sandra (*sardonically*) Thank you, Phillip. And goodbye.

Phillip exits

Goodbye.

Norman (*emerging from his room*) Has he gone?

Sandra (*nodding*) He's gone. Do you know something? Tomorrow you'll beg my forgiveness. And I'd forgive you, of course. The only trouble is—I shan't be here. (*She quickly goes into her room and stuffs a few personal items into a small suitcase*)

He stands watching her unbelievingly

Norman What?

She doesn't answer. He is quietly fearful

Sandra, what are you doing? Sandra! Say something. Speak to me. You're in pain.

Sandra That's not pain. It's hilarity. It's about the stupidity, the ridiculousness of men.

Norman What can I do?

Sandra Thank you. You've done enough.

Norman (*a thought*) Hold on! You haven't arranged to meet him somewhere? Have you?

Act II, Scene 2

Sandra No. I have not arranged to meet him. He is out of my life. And you are out of my life. Thank God.
Norman Stop playing games and I'll play Sinatra. That'll restore us. (*He plays Sinatra on CD*)

Sinatra sings "Young At Heart"

Sandra, you can never get away from me. Can you? Sandra!
Sandra I can be contacted at this number. (*She hands him a note*)
Norman What are you doing? Where the hell you going?
Sandra I shall be staying with Bernice for a few days.
Norman And after that? After that——
Sandra Norman, in the midst of death we are in life. Nothing's certain.
Norman You're not leaving me.
Sandra Yes, I am, Norman. I'm leaving now.
Norman I won't let you. (*He bars the door*)
Sandra Yes, you will Norman. (*She picks up the "I Ching" and packs that as well*)
Norman It doesn't belong to you.

She laughs, packs it and closes her case

Sandra Norman, be a good boy.
Norman You're just trying to scare me.
Sandra Goodbye Norman!
Norman Think you can change? Sandra! Think you can be someone else? Your time of life?
Sandra Who knows?
Norman Please don't leave me Sandra. Mr Sinatra won't like it. Please?

She doesn't reply

Good girl! (*Now like a showman with an American accent*) And now Miss Sandra Lewis! This question carries a prize of one million dollars——
Sandra It's over Norman. It's all over. (*She takes up the remote control, turns Sinatra off and throws the control across the room*) I'm finished with it all.
Norman What was the name of the sad song that Frank Sinatra sang in the Film *Anchors Aweigh*?
Sandra "I Fall In Love Too Easily".
Norman The jackpot! (*He gestures, singing the song, becoming Sinatra*)
Sandra Thanks.
Norman You love me too much.
Sandra Far too much.
Norman I'm dreaming this.
Sandra Norman. The game's over.
Norman Sandra! Before you go. You know what you need? You need a back massage. (*He grabs her throat with two hands and pushes her towards the floor*) 'Cos he's got high hopes, he's got high hopes, he's got you deep in the heart of me and deep in the heart—Something's gotta give. (*He is now on top of her, his body rhythmically moving slowly backward and*

forwards, against her, in a frightening sexual motion) Something's gotta give. It's quite the life to play gypsy and roam—until your heart goes wap! And all at once you're hooked, you're cooked—you're part of the tender trap. No more packing and unpacking—get my slippers—make a pizza. You can go to extremes with impossible dreams but it's so much nicer to come home. Sandra, tell me you love it. (*He holds her by the throat, his arms outstretched*)

Sandra hardly struggles, but just stares up at him with stark eyes

Dirty. Dirty. (*This very quiet, but then he suddenly lets her go, sits on the floor and cries*) The monster. He loved that girl. It was the one pure golden thing in his life. But he went too far, didn't he? Sandra. Please call the doctor.
Sandra Norman! I'm at a loss.
Norman Please save me from myself. Hey! I know! We'll go out tonight. We'll go to the opera.

She goes to the door with her case. He still sits on the floor and talks quietly

Sandra ... (*It is a plea for help, from the depths of despair*)
Sandra Norman, I can't swim. How can I save anyone if I can't even save myself? Darling, what else can I say?
Norman You care too much to leave me.
Sandra I don't care any more.
Norman If you don't care—why are you crying?
Sandra (*in a mock Hollywood pose*) I'm not crying baby, don't kid yourself.
Norman You can't get away from Frankie. (*He sings a few lines from "All The Way"*)
Sandra I'm not playing Sinatra any more. I've grown out of him.
Norman You can't. Frankie won't let you go. There's no future without him.
Sandra You're dead right. The future's too terrible to contemplate.
Norman Ah, you admit there's no escape.
Sandra Norman, even so you have to try. What did he say? "It's a circus. But where are the clowns?—" I loved him. (*She fixes an extreme smile on her face*) Going for your sake but mainly for mine. It strikes me you'll survive. Instant Norman, reconstituted by microwave. It's me I'm concerned about. Survival! That's the secret. That's what I loved most about old friend Frank. Him! Survival. But I think he can manage without me from now on.

She quickly departs, slamming the door in his face

He rushes out, calling, after her

Norman (*as he goes*) SANDRA! SANDRA! DON'T LEAVE ME. PLEASE DON'T LEAVE ME. SANDRA! SANDRA!

But soon he returns, and sits down

At last. She's gone at last. (*He laughs. But then starts smashing things, hurling plates across the room and his birthday cake against the wall. He*

Act II, Scene 2

takes a wooden work mallet, growls at his reflection in the mirror, and smashes the mirror to smithereens. He picks up the telephone) No more! No more! No more! (*He yanks the wire from the socket, stamps on the telephone. He goes quiet, crosses over to his workbench, and stares into space*

There is a passage of time. It is now dark in the room. Norman is crouched in a foetal position on his workbench. There is a ring on the doorbell

Norman goes to the door and opens it. He returns to the room, followed a few seconds later by Phillip, who stays in the doorway. He is not at all surprised that Phillip is there, although he has not been expecting him

Phillip (*producing a chicken from inside his coat and holding it up*) I came by a chicken. It's organic. May I come in? (*He comes into the room*)
Norman (*taking the chicken*) It's real. It's unchilled food.
Phillip Yes. Just for a change.
Norman She took your book. *The Book of Change*. The *I Ching*. She's gone. She believes she can start a new life. What do you want, Phillip?
Phillip I've used up all my chances. Only you can save me.

Being in a position of power is a new experience for Norman. He likes it

Norman Sit down. Over there.
Phillip Yes, Norman. I realized that we had so much in common; that you would never turn me away. I could never dream of wanting anything else. Of being anywhere else—I—I ... (*He has run out of words*)
Norman Carry on.
Phillip All my life I never had a chance. But you see right through me, and that's what I need, that's my salvation. Only the truth can save me. I want to be truthful, because I have no choice. I'm hollow. I want to live for the moment. Teach me. I have done the most despicable things in my life. Stabbed my best friends in the back. But you Norman, you are always expecting the thrust. That's wonderful. So please don't cast me out. We'll play such games. "I remember as a child I walked and talked as a child, but when I became a man I put away childish things——"
Norman "Though I speak with the tongues of men and of angels, and have not charity, I am become as sounding brass——". I hate charity. When they come to the door I spit in their boxes. She won't tell Dr Sinclair, will she? I'm so pleased she's out of danger. Besides, hurting her solves nothing. Do you think she'll ever forgive me?
Phillip As eggs are eggs.
Norman Anyway, that's God's job, forgiving.
Phillip Exactly. Can I get you something?
Norman Yes please. Some milk.
Phillip So, may I stay? A few days? A few weeks? I just need somewhere to rest my head and cut out the crap and start again. Please?

Phillip, about to get the milk, is interrupted

Norman Are your hands clean?

Phillip shows his hands

Good boy. Phillip, whoever you are, do you solemnly vow to do food shopping at Marks and Spencer's every Friday?
Phillip I do.
Norman And go to the Post Office and post my parcels every Monday morning.
Phillip Gladly.
Norman And bring me hot buttered toast and thick marmalade every Sunday morning until the end of the world?
Phillip I swear.
Norman Then you may enter my kingdom. Because I'm the king of the castle. Take off your shoes.

Phillip does so

No! Second thoughts! Put them on again.

Phillip complies, then gets a glass of milk from the kitchen cupboard. Norman inspects the chicken

How clever of you to come by a chicken. I know, we'll have coq au vin for dinner tonight. With steamed broccoli and pommes sauté. And some Crêpes Suzette with honey. Yes?
Phillip Sounds wonderful. I'll prepare the vegetables. I'm good at vegetables. Here's your milk.
Norman Thank you, Phillip.
Phillip My pleasure. You know, this is the perfect house. It's the only place to be. (*He sinks into an armchair and flips through a book*)
Norman I'll start cooking soon. Is that all right?
Phillip You're the boss.
Norman (*realisation dawning quietly*) Yes. I'm the boss. I know, for a change, let's play Sinatra.
Phillip What a wonderful idea.
Norman (*shouting*) Well, move yourself then!

Phillip jumps up, goes to the radiogram and puts on a record. Sinatra sings "Young At Heart"

She thinks she can change. Do you know Phillip, nothing changes. Nothing changes all the time.

They both sway as they watch Sinatra going round and around

CURTAIN

FURNITURE AND PROPERTY LIST

ACT I

Scene 1

On stage: Living-room:
Fireplace with mantelpiece
3-piece suite
Sideboards and various cupboards. *On them*: Chinese vases, bottle of cherry brandy, glasses
Small tables
Sofa table. *On it:* remote control for CD
Chairs
Bureau. *In it:* trick dagger. *On it:* books, telephone
Radiogram. *On turntable:* record. *In cabinet:* records, mainly Sinatra
CD player with amplifier and speakers. *By it:* CDs, mainly Sinatra
Workbench. *On it:* bookbinding materials, antique volumes, tools including hammer and wooden mallet, packing materials
Bookcase. *On shelves:* books.
On walls: posters and photos of Frank Sinatra, Russian and Persian wall-hangings, old prints, mirror, Sinatra hat on hook
TV and video
Deep cupboard. *In it:* food, microwave

Norman's bedroom:
Bed with pillows and bedding. *Under bed*: glossy magazines
Bedside table
Wardrobe. *In it:* clothes, coat, hat, scarf
Key in door

Sandra's bedroom:
Bed with bedding
Bedside cupboard. *In it:* photo album
Wardrobe. *In it:* clothes, hats, shoes. *On top:* small suitcase
Mirror on wall

Off stage: Handbag containing notebook **(Sandra)**

Personal: **Norman:** wrist-watch (required throughout)

Scene 2

Strike: Food packages, cutlery, glasses

Set: Food packages in kitchen cupboard
Meringues and cream in kitchen cupboard
Mug on workbench
Mozart record on radiogram

Off stage: Handbag containing notebook **(Sandra)**
Food packages and cutlery **(Norman)**
Copy of *I Ching* **(Phillip)**
Tray with 2 mugs of tea, plate of biscuits **(Sandra)**
Meringue with cream **(Norman)**

Personal: **Norman:** poem in pocket
Sandra: letter in coat pocket

ACT II

Scene 1

Strike: Dirty mugs, plate of biscuits
Food packages, cutlery
Letter, handbag

Re-set: *I Ching* on Sandra's bedside table

Off stage: Birthday cake and knife **(Norman)**
Empty milk bottle **(Sandra)**
Bottle of milk **(Sandra)**
Tray with 3 mugs of tea **(Sandra)**

Personal: **Norman:** poem in pocket
Phillip: wrist-watch

Scene 2

Strike: Cake, tray with tea, etc.

Set: Mahler record on radiogram

During Black-out on page 30, set:
Balloons on mantelpieces
"Happy Birthday Norman" on mirror
Table laid for party with party hats, birthday cake, knife, etc.
Wrapped present of stuffed owl under Sandra's bed

Off stage: Bags of shopping **(Norman** and **Sandra)**
Handbag with birthday card **(Sandra)**
Box of chocolates **(Phillip)**
Chicken **(Phillip)**
Glass of milk **(Phillip)**

Personal: **Norman:** Building Society book in pocket
Sandra: note in pocket

LIGHTING PLOT

Property fittings required: wall-brackets in living-room, lights in bedrooms
Interior. A living-room with 2 bedrooms off. The same scene throughout

ACT I, SCENE 1   Evening

To open: Black-out

Cue 1	When ready *Bring up general lighting, wall-brackets, bedroom lights on*	(Page 1)
Cue 2	As **Norman** and **Sandra** dance *Fade to Black-out*	(Page 7)
Cue 3	When ready *Bring up general lighting as before*	(Page 7)
Cue 4	**Norman** switches off the lights *Cut lighting to three-quarters*	(Page 8)
Cue 5	**Sandra** gets into bed *Black-out*	(Page 9)

ACT I, SCENE 2   Late morning

To open: General lighting

No cues

ACT II, SCENE 1   Afternoon

To open: General lighting

| Cue 6 | **Norman** twirls Sandra around
Fade to Black-out | (Page 27) |

ACT II, SCENE 2   Night, then afternoon and evening

To open: Wall-brackets on; dim lighting in bedrooms

Cue 7	**Norman** and **Sandra** lie on their beds *Black-out*	(Page 30)
Cue 8	When ready *Bring up general lighting—day*	(Page 30)
Cue 9	**Norman** crosses to his workbench and stares into space *Fade lights to denote passage of time, then dim evening lighting*	(Page 41)

EFFECTS PLOT

ACT I

Cue 1	**Norman:** "I just like to hear it." *Ping from microwave*	(Page 5)
Cue 2	**Sandra** presses remote control at CD player *Music: Sinatra "That Old Black Magic"*	(Page 5)
Cue 3	**Sandra** turns Sinatra off *Cut music*	(Page 5)
Cue 4	**Sandra** starts record on radiogram *Music: Sinatra "Young at Heart"*	(Page 7)
Cue 5	As **Norman** and **Sandra** dance *Fade music*	(Page 7)
Cue 6	After a short time lapse *Music: Sinatra "Strangers in the Night"*	(Page 7)
Cue 7	**Norman** suddenly switches off music *Cut music*	(Page 7)
Cue 8	**Norman:** "Thank you very much." (*He takes off his hat*) *Dogs barking, getting louder and louder, then subsiding*	(Page 8)
Cue 9	**Norman** presses CD remote control *Music: Sinatra "The Tender Trap"*	(Page 8)
Cue 10	**Norman** switches off CD *Cut music*	(Page 8)
Cue 11	Black-out *Dogs bark, phone rings three times*	(Page 9)
Cue 12	As Scene 2 opens *Music: Mozart*	(Page 10)
Cue 13	**Norman** takes Mozart record off *Cut music*	(Page 10)
Cue 14	**Sandra** presses remote control at CD *Music: Sinatra "Come Fly With Me"*	(Page 12)
Cue 15	**Sandra:** "Yes, isn't that beautiful?" *Microwave pings*	(Page 12)
Cue 16	**Sandra:** "What would I do without you?" *Doorbell rings*	(Page 12)
Cue 17	**Norman:** "It's never to your advantage." *Doorbell rings*	(Page 13)

Playing Sinatra 47

Cue 18	**Sandra:** "Who can that be?" *Cut music*	(Page 12)
Cue 19	**Norman** presses remote control at CD *Music: Sinatra "I've Got You Under My Skin"*	(Page 13)
Cue 20	**Sandra** turns off CD *Cut music*	(Page 13)
Cue 21	**Norman** takes **Sandra**'s coat to her room *Telephone rings*	(Page 15)
Cue 22	**Sandra** plays a record on the radiogram *Music: Sinatra "High Hopes"*	(Page 19)
Cue 23	**Norman** turns up volume *Increase volume of music*	(Page 19)

ACT II

Cue 24	**Norman** (*singing*): "Happy birthday to me——" (*2nd time*) *Telephone rings*	(Page 20)
Cue 25	**Norman** plays Sinatra on CD *Music: Sinatra "Young at Heart"*	(Page 20)
Cue 26	**Norman** turns off music *Cut music*	(Page 20)
Cue 27	**Norman** plays Sinatra on CD *Music: Sinatra "Young at Heart"*	(Page 21)
Cue 28	**Sandra** turns off music *Cut music*	(Page 21)
Cue 29	**Phillip** puts record on radiogram *Music: Sinatra "You Make Me Feel So Young"*	(Page 24)
Cue 30	**Phillip** stops record *Cut music*	(Page 24)
Cue 31	**Norman** puts record on radiogram *Music: Sinatra "Come Fly With Me"*	(Page 27)
Cue 32	As Scene 2 opens *Music: Mahler*	(Page 27)
Cue 33	**Norman** stops music *Cut Mahler*	(Page 27)
Cue 34	**Norman** plays Sinatra on CD *Music: Sinatra "All The Way"*	(Page 27)
Cue 35	**Norman** switches off CD *Cut music*	(Page 27)
Cue 36	**Phillip** presses remote control at CD *Music: Sinatra "All the Way"*	(Page 27)
Cue 37	**Phillip** switches on CD *Music: Sinatra "Something's Gotta Give"*	(Page 29)

Cue 38	**Sandra** and **Norman** lie on their beds. Black-out *Dogs bark, telephone rings three times. Children's voices sing "Happy Birthday"*	(Page 30)
Cue 39	**Sandra** plays record on radiogram *Music: Sinatra "Come Fly With Me"*	(Page 31)
Cue 40	**Sandra** turns off radiogram *Cut music*	(Page 31)
Cue 41	**Norman** presses remote control at CD *Music: Sinatra "Young at Heart"*	(Page 33)
Cue 42	**Norman** and **Sandra** sit back in silence *Long pause, then ring on doorbell*	(Page 34)
Cue 43	**Sandra:** "... that's all that matters." *Doorbell rings*	(Page 34)
Cue 44	**Sandra** turns off CD *Cut music*	(Page 34)
Cue 45	**Norman:** "... anything come between us." *Doorbell rings*	(Page 34)
Cue 46	**Norman** switches on CD *Music: Sinatra "Fools Rush In"*	(Page 36)
Cue 47	**Norman** turns off CD *Cut music*	(Page 36)
Cue 48	**Norman** presses remote control at CD *Music: Sinatra "Fools Rush In"*	(Page 37)
Cue 49	**Sandra** turns off CD *Cut music*	(Page 37)
Cue 50	**Norman** switches on CD *Music: Sinatra "Young at Heart"*	(Page 39)
Cue 51	**Sandra** presses remote control at CD *Cut music*	(Page 39)
Cue 52	**Norman** crouches in foetal position *Doorbell rings*	(Page 41)
Cue 53	**Phillip** puts record on radiogram *Music: Sinatra "Young at Heart"*	(Page 42)

MADE AND PRINTED IN GREAT BRITAIN BY
LATIMER TREND & COMPANY LTD PLYMOUTH

MADE IN ENGLAND